Holidays are fun! Everybody knows that. But holidays can also be times of pressure, fatigue, and even boredom. While many are involved in merrymaking, others slip into frustration and even despair.

The good news of this book is that we can learn to control the holidays, instead of letting the holidays control us. We can learn to handle the holidays and to enjoy them—even if the world around us seems to have been caught in a swirl of maddening activities.

How do we handle holidays? That is what the following pages are all about!

A PSYCHOLOGIST'S GUIDE TO
TURNING YOUR HECTIC HOLIDAYS
INTO TRUE CELEBRATIONS

HANDLING THE HOLIDAYS

GARY R. COLLINS

Ventura, CA U.S.A.

The foreign language publishing of all Vision House books is under the direction of GLINT. GLINT provides financial and technical help for the adaptation, translation, and publishing of books for millions of people worldwide. For information regarding translation, contact: GLINT, P.O. Box 6688, Ventura, California 93006.

Published by Vision House
Ventura, California 93006
Printed in U.S.A.

Library of Congress Cataloging in Publication Data

Collins, Gary R.
Handling the holidays.

Rev. ed of: Coping with Christmas. c1975.
1. Christmas. 2. Christmas—Psychological aspects.
I. Title.
BV45.C59 1982 263'.91 82-15807
ISBN 0-88449-088-2

Contents

1

The Move Toward Christmas

There was a time, many years ago, when Christmas was celebrated only in December. Wreaths went up at mid-month, the tree was decorated a few days before the twenty-fifth (and in some homes not until Christmas Eve), and on New Year's Day all of the decorations were taken down to be stored neatly in the old attic until next year.

But that was long ago, and far different from the way we celebrate holidays today.

Department stores design their Christmas

advertising a year in advance; merchants order their Christmas supplies around Easter; magazine editors send their holiday editions to press before Labor Day, and by Halloween, Santa Claus has made his annual appearance along with the ghosts, goblins, and witches. Long before Thanksgiving the post office urges us to "mail early," and a lot of kids start making their "Christmas want lists" even before the autumn leaves have turned to magnificent fall colors.

When Christmas comes so early, is it surprising that some have called this annual celebration a time of madness rather than merriment? Have we made holiday times so busy and so commercial that we have taken away much of the fun? Have we loaded ourselves with so many chores that Christmas has become a time when we talk about peace but feel mostly pressure? Is the celebration of Christ's birth more a wearisome burden than a time for relaxed fellowship with good friends and good food?

And is Thanksgiving any more relaxed?

What about Easter, summer vacations, or the Fourth of July?

Everybody has heard of Ebenezer Scrooge. He hated Christmas and apparently wasn't inclined to enjoy holidays of any sort. He could have written the above paragraphs and gone through the rest of his life mumbling, "Bah! Humbug!"

But Scrooge changed, and so can we!

Let's agree that in many ways the holidays have become too commercialized, too pressured, too demanding, even boring. That doesn't mean that we must slip into frustration and an attitude of despair. We can control the holidays, instead of letting the holidays control us. We can learn to handle the holidays and to enjoy them—even if the world around us seems to have been caught in a swirl of maddening activities.

How do we handle holidays? That is what the following pages are all about!

2

The Meaning of Christmas

WHEN you think of Christmas, what comes to your mind? Perhaps you think of things like:

DECORATIONS: holly and Christmas trees, sparkling tinsel, and colored lights;

GIFTS: new toys, surprises, brightly wrapped boxes, and packages in the mail;

FOOD: turkey and cranberry sauce, hot rolls, plum pudding, mince pie, or Christmas cookies;

PARTIES: good times, singing, visits with friends;

RELIGION: massive choirs, candlelight

services, Christmas carols and chrèces;
MEMORIES: Grandma's house, waiting for Santa Claus, believing in elves and flying reindeer.

It would be nice if we could stop at this point, thinking of Christmas as an annual winter fantasy which everyone enjoys. But Christmas also has a darker side. For many people it means:

FRANTIC BUSYNESS: trying to get the shopping done, the presents wrapped, the tree up, the cards mailed, the baking done—all before an inflexible deadline known as December 25;
FATIGUE: missed sleep, late nights, and frenzied schedules, all making us edgy and inclined to explode in anger or irritation even over little things;
FRUSTRATION: finding appropriate gifts, trying to pay for presents we can't really afford, trying to fit all of our social events into the calendar;
FIERCE LONELINESS that comes when we are away from loved ones, or worse, when we have no loved ones.

FEAR that Dad will drink too much at the office party, that the kids will complain about their presents, or that the family dinner party will disintegrate into arguing and bickering.

There is also a problem about the things we are supposed to believe. Everyone knows that Santa Claus and Rudolph are make believe, but how do we handle the virgin birth, the singing angels, or the story of so-called wise men traveling hundreds of miles to bring costly gifts to a pauper's baby whom they didn't even know? These events, which are supposed to have given Christmas its start in the first place, are pretty difficult for modern, rational people to accept.

Christmas, therefore, becomes for most of us a mixture of fantasies and frustrations, a merging of pleasure with pressure. Little wonder, therefore, that Christmas has been called "a sick holiday," "a crazy time of year," "an insane event." One psychiatrist has expressed it concisely:

> Any celebration that sets up such unrealistic, magical expectations is very unfair to human beings. People are pushed to deny the reality of their own lives—their financial situation, their true relationships. There is almost a delusional mood. This is not the celebration of humanity, but a delusion, a myth. It is a very primitive holiday.
>
> The rest of the year, we talk about being open and honest with each other, but for a couple of weeks we're supposed to deny—to act crazy—to

> pretend that we love everyone, that we're financially able to do things we know we can't do, that we have a great relationship with the kids. That's crazy. It's madness.[1]

Somehow it hardly seems that this was part of God's plan when He sent His Son to be born in a Bethlehem manger. The people who participated in that first Christmas kept the celebration simple. Mary, the teenaged mother of the baby, rejoiced; the shepherds, well-established working men, took off an hour or so from work and then went back to the job with a new gratitude to God; the wise men, scholars and intellectuals who also must have been wealthy, sought for the child, worshiped Him, and went home; Simeon and Anna, the aged senior citizens, rejoiced in the child's coming, then waited for death to take them to their ultimate destiny. In our day things are more complicated. Christmas has become a frantic winter holiday—so frantic, in fact, that perhaps millions of celebrating people miss the whole point of Christmas. They are celebrating and are not even sure why.

3

The Missing of Christmas

HAVE you ever missed a television program that you wanted to see, or forgotten an appointment that you had planned to keep? In such situations we usually respond with disappointment, but this doesn't always happen when people miss Christmas. Every December great numbers of us get caught up in yuletide activities and fail to realize that we are missing the real meaning of all the festivities.

Missing Christmas is nothing new. Even on that day when Jesus was born centuries ago, some people in the little town of Bethlehem missed the event altogether.[2] There was, for example, the innkeeper. He missed Christmas because he was too caught up in his business. Surely this was a prosperous time for the innkeeper. Bethlehem was filled with citizens who had come to pay their taxes, the inn was full to overflowing and the innkeeper was so busy with his business that he pretty much ignored the birth of the Christ child nearby.

Things are not too different today. For many, Christmas 'tis the season to make money, attract customers, and make sales. There is, of course, nothing wrong with this buying and selling. Business keeps the economy afloat, and from this everyone benefits. We can get so caught up in the commercial aspects of Christmas, however, that we completely overlook the poor babe of Bethlehem whose coming provided the whole reason for Christmas in the first place.

The busy innkeeper was not the only one who missed Christmas. The residents of his hotel must have missed the birth of Christ because they were too comfortable as they slept only a few feet away from an earth-changing event. These people were respectable citizens. They had come to be registered, and perhaps some of them had turned this government requirement into a reason for vacationing. But they still missed Christmas! Today many good citizens are enjoying life and are too comfortable to realize that they might have need for a Savior. The Christ of Bethlehem seemingly has no relevance for them, so they have eliminated Him from their holiday celebrations.

Another who missed Christmas was King Herod. Business and comfort were not his problem; the king missed Christmas because he was too much concerned with his own career and personal advancement. Herod was a cunning, ruthless man who reportedly murdered a host of people including his own wife and three sons. It is unlikely that Herod had any personal religious beliefs, but he was threatened by the news of a "newborn king" and he determined to assassinate the young Jesus as quickly as possible.

Numerous psychological studies have shown that people tend to be pretty self-centered. Many of us are reluctant, perhaps afraid, to help others in time of need, so we go through life as little islands, looking to our own interests and minding our own business. Like Herod, we are aware of the birth of Christ, but we miss the significance of this event because of our self-interest, greed, search for security, or struggles for significance. Jesus just isn't important to people who are self-centered and looking out for their own interests.

There was one other group of people who missed the first Christmas. Of all people, these men should have known better because they were the religious leaders. They claimed to be followers of God, they knew all about the Bible, and they even were able to tell Herod where the Jewish Messiah would be born. But these people missed Christmas because they were too religious, too caught up in theology to see Christ's significance to their own lives.

There are people today who know all about the fine points of theology and are experts in Bible knowledge, but they have no personal hunger for God, no joy, no peace, no vital relationship with the Christ whose birth was heralded on that first Christmas. Ask them a Bible question and they will give the right answer, but they have no intimate contact with the Bible's author.

In the Western world most people put up and decorate a tree in their home at Christmastime. Nobody knows for sure how this custom got started. Perhaps it began with the Romans who, on festive occasions, used to decorate their houses with tree branches to bring good luck. The English took over this custom at Christmas, decorating with holly and ivy, but the use of an entire tree probably started on the European continent. Many have traced the custom to Martin Luther who, it is said, saw the Christmas tree as a symbol of life, pointing to heaven and decorated with candles to symbolize Christ's coming as the light of the world.

Beneath the lights and tinsel, however, most Christmas trees are dead. They have been cut off from their roots and will be thrown

into the fire early in January. Artificial trees will be packed away, of course, but they have been lifeless from the beginning.

A lot of people are like Christmas trees. They get all spruced up at Christmas, decorate their homes and businesses, and even hang wreaths in their churches. But underneath all of the tinsel and decorations they are dead, joyless, bored people. Surrounded and entwined by the symbols of Christmas, they are putting on a happy front, trying not to let the world and themselves see that they have missed the whole point of the celebration.

4

The Madness of Christmas

"MADNESS" implies something psychological—a form of insanity characterized by great excitement, enthusiasm, and busyness. Little children, of course, get excited about Christmas and some older people even get enthusiastic, but almost everybody gets busy, so busy that we at least feel at times on the verge of insanity. In December, business people are at the height of their sales activity; the post office is swamped with packages, cards, and impatient customers; students are pushing to get papers written and exams taken before heading home for the holidays; airlines are booked to capacity and the terminals are crowded; churches have a number of special meetings and Christmas programs; and people like us get caught up in a whirl of holiday preparations.

Why is this season so hectic? Busyness is almost a trademark of our current age, but the pressure and activity seem especially intense at Christmas. One of the reasons for this, it would seem, is that we are too much caught up with the expectations of others. Everyone is expected to send cards at Christmas, keep up family traditions, visit relatives, host parties, bake "goodies," buy gifts, and set a table like those pictured in the "better homes" magazines. If we fail to meet these expectations, we risk being criticized, and this is threatening. So we rush around, driven by what we think other people, including our children, are expecting from us.

Might it be, however, that others do not expect as much from us as we sometimes think? Perhaps a lot of the madness of

Christmas is self-imposed. We blame others for pressuring us, but it may be closer to the truth to admit that we are pressuring ourselves, pushing ourselves to do a whole host of things which really do not need to be done. Over the years we may have slowly assimilated a variety of expectations into our lives, setting up standards which now are almost impossible to keep.

There is a reason for this self-driving attitude. Busyness can produce problems but it can also hide problems. If we are busy, we can feel harried and at odds with our families or fellow employees, but if we are busy, we can also avoid facing the real difficulties of life. The busy man, for example, has an excuse for not dealing with the developing problems in his marriage or for not spending time with his demanding children. By keeping busy he lulls himself into thinking that he is very important, and he finds that there is no time to deal with the painful problems which may be lurking behind the mask of hyperactivity.

Might it be, therefore, that this busyness at

Christmas is at least partially defensive? Perhaps busyness is a technique which people use subconsciously to keep from facing the real emptiness, lack of peace, or inner disappointments in their lives. Christmas is a time when we hear a lot about peace, joy, and love. If we have no inner peace, joy, or love, we avoid facing this painful reality by keeping ourselves too busy to think.

One way to cope with the Christmas madness is to slow down deliberately. This is risky. If we allow time for reflection at Christmas, we might be freed to realize that our lives and marriages are not as successful as we would like. We might realize that we are too status oriented, too much ruled by the expectations of others, and not nearly so happy at Christmas as the carol singers and department store advertisements might imply.

To slow down in a fast-paced society and at the most hectic season of the year is not only risky, however. It is extremely difficult. It puts us out of step with everyone else. If we cut back on our Christmas card list or decorating activities, we get criticized for hating Christmas, not appreciating our friends, or being a Scrooge. There is also the possibility of our developing an attitude of smug superiority. "Look at me," we say to the world by our actions, "I'm not pressured by Christmas like you are!"

But the situation is not hopeless. The answer to Christmas madness can be found in three not-so-little words: balance, meditation, and priorities.

There needs, first, to be *balance* in our Christmas activities. We need not go overboard in hectic activities, but neither do we take all the fun out of the season by refusing to celebrate. Christmas is a festival, the anniversary of Christ's birth. Christians especially should not ignore the festival, but neither should we be overwhelmed and frazzled by it. Perhaps Christians should lead the way in showing how Christmas can be commemorated in an enjoyable but less harried way.

This brings us to our second suggestion,

meditation. It is time we reevaluate Christmas—how we spend the month of December and what our spending patterns are at this time of year. When we get really busy, we often find ourselves fatigued, irritable, discouraged, and too active with other things to spend time thinking about God. In our haste we scribble "Merry Xmas." This is a shortcut for busy people, but it also takes the Christ out of Christmas. That is what always happens when Christmas is too busy—Christ gets left out.[3]

The people who celebrated the first Christmas did not appear to be busy. It's true that the shepherds went to the manger "with haste," but we see no evidence in them or anyone else of a hectic life-style. Perhaps at Christmas we should be still and contemplate that Christ is God—come in the flesh to change the lives even of busy twentieth-century people.

How we do this is suggested by our third basic word, *priorities*. We can't do everything that we want to do at Christmas and still feel relaxed, so perhaps we shouldn't try. Instead, let's decide what is most important. There will be individual differences in this direction. Not everyone can trim the Christmas card list, avoid visits with relatives, or refrain from putting up a tree, but each family or individual can decide what *has* to be done and what they would *like* to do but could avoid this year if necessary.

Every Christmas it seems that our mailboxes contain a number of appeals for money. Most of the causes are worthy, but few of us can give to every organization that asks, so we set up priorities, giving a large gift to one, a smaller gift to another, and perhaps no gifts to the remainder. In a similar way, with the Christmas demands on our time we must decide what is most important and cut back on the rest. Only in this way will we control Christmas instead of letting Christmas control and pressure us.

5

The Misery of Christmas

CHRISTMAS, as everybody knows, is a time to be merry. It is a time for parties, gaiety, good food, gifts, traditions, carols, and happy expressions of peace and good wishes for the coming new year. We think about shepherds rejoicing, angels announcing "good tidings of great joy," and Mary "magnifying and praising God" for the coming of the Christ child. Enthusiastic anticipation, exciting activity, pleasant memories, and warm feelings all merge into something called "the Christmas spirit."

But great numbers of people experience Christmas very differently. For them, the season to be jolly is instead a time of discouragement and deep unhappiness. Suicide rates jump sharply in the days surrounding Christmas, accidents and fires are common, and even people who rejoice in the activity and message of Christmas sometimes find themselves facing what has come to be known as the Christmas depression.[4] This Christmas depression is not something which is completely new. Psychiatrists have known about it for years. What is new is that people are recognizing how common and widespread this condition is.

When Jesus was born in Judea, the country wasn't bursting with happy people. The populace was in the process of being taxed by a foreign emperor. Even at the time of Christ's birth some people were planning a revolution which was to erupt a few years later. When King Herod heard of the nativity, he was troubled, the Bible says, and all Jerusalem with him. When he failed to trick the wise men into revealing Christ's whereabouts, Herod authorized a mass murder of all male children two years of age and under. Mary, Joseph, and the Christ child escaped to Egypt with their lives, but the whole town of Bethlehem was plunged into weeping and great mourning. It appears, therefore, that in spite of the joy on that first Christmas night, there was also what one writer has called a "dark side of Christmas."[5] This dark side still exists and makes Christmas a miserable time for many people.

Why are some people miserable and depressed at Christmas? There are several reasons. First, many people experience *loneliness* at Christmas. Students, servicemen, and others who are away from home; divorced people, widows and those who grieve (especially on the first Christmas without a loved one); the sick and elderly; people who feel unloved and friendless—all tend to feel discouraged and lonely when everyone else is preparing for parties or visits with friends and relatives. Even people who have no problems with loneliness during the rest of the year are likely to feel unhappy and rejected when they have no one with whom to share the joys of Christmas. Sometimes this leads to self-pity or a "poor-little-me" attitude, to resentment at being left out, and to envy of those who appear to be happy at the holiday season. For people who are alone, without friends or family, life seems to stop at Christmas. The streets are deserted, the stores are all closed, and the unwanted solitude is almost unbearable.

Second, *disappointment* is common at Christmas. Caught up in the enthusiasm of the season we sometimes develop unrealistic expectations about how happy Christmas will be, how much we will receive, how much fun we will have, how much the kids will like the toys we have stretched our budgets to buy, how a husband will keep his promise to stay sober. Helped by the media and the superlatives of eager merchants, we set our hopes very high, so high in fact that we are almost assured of disappointment.

Sometimes this leads to the bitterness that was expressed by one mother in a Christmas Eve article written for a midwestern newspaper. "I hate Christmas," she wrote:

I have thoughts of getting everything ready and then disappearing on Christmas Eve. I am sure my family would be happier without me, but I haven't got the money for Mexico, or even Milwaukee. (Actually, at this time of year I would prefer Israel.) So I stay and make everyone miserable.

Because I suffer from the holiday syndrome . . . I have thought a great deal about it, its cause and its cure. Its cause is the unreal anticipation of events and emotions that people expect to happen but which rarely do because they are expected. . . . Its cure is not to expect anything, except the worst: crying, disappointed children who break toys at the rate of at least three an hour; irate, bill paying husbands who want to be left alone to watch football; friends bearing sticky Christmas cookies decorated by their crying disappointed children. Then you can feel not disappointed and disillusioned, but vindicated and superior.

> The only thing I have against Scrooge is that he copped out, gave in, went over to the side of sweetness and light.[6]

What a bitter, cynical attitude! Disappointed over past Christmases, this lady has made a deliberate decision to expect nothing but disappointments in the future, and because of her attitude she is likely to experience exactly what she expects. She, and others like her, once anticipated so much at Christmas that they were disappointed and miserable. Now they expect nothing and they're still miserable.

Third, *feelings of inadequacy* are usually accentuated at this time of year. Two psychiatrists, one in Europe and one in the United States, reported that most of their Christmas patients are people who felt inadequate and unwanted as children. Over the years these feelings become buried in the subconscious, but they rise to the surface when people begin to compare themselves to the perfect Christ child, whom everyone wanted, worshiped, and adored. Some people feel inadequate because they cannot entertain as well as their friends, saddened because they cannot afford the gifts they would like to give their children, frustrated because they cannot give presents that are as expensive as those they have received, or guilty because they have overlooked someone or received a gift they feel is undeserved.

Recently a Chicago radio station invited listeners to call in their observations about Christmas depression. After one or two calls from people who smugly condemned others for becoming discouraged at Christmas, an elderly grandmother phoned the station, "My husband and I are retired," she volunteered, "and we don't have enough money to buy gifts for all of the grandchildren. All of their other grandparents do buy gifts, so the children assume *we* don't love them." The lady was crying when she finished her story. Apparently she was a dedicated Christian but she was miserable at Christmas because she couldn't give. The only person sadder than a child with an empty stocking on

Christmas morning is the parent or grandparent who is unable to fill it!

A fourth cause of yuletide misery is *memories* of Christmases gone by. The holiday season often triggers reminders of Christmases in the past when an accident caused suffering or death, a drunken outburst brought misery or toppled the Christmas tree, a Christmas play turned to embarrassment when we forgot our lines, a Christmas morning turned to sadness when someone was sick or unemployed.

In addition to these sad memories there are thoughts of happy times which, regretfully, have gone forever. Christmas reminds us of experiences which can never be repeated because a loved one is gone, the children have grown, or old customs have faded.

Probably there are other reasons for Christmas depression. The children, for example, become excited, less controllable and so much more on our nerves that we explode in outbursts of anger, after which we feel enraged and angry with ourselves. Sometimes we feel guilty for not buying more expensive presents, or for not sharing

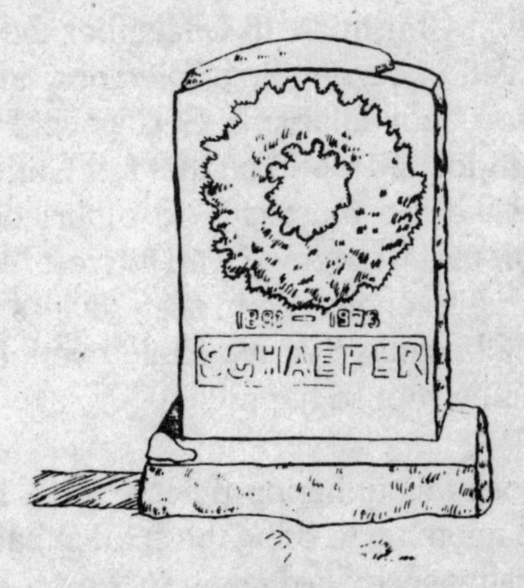

Christmas with someone who is needy. Then there are the traditional family gatherings where old resentments, old rivalries, and old insecurities, which we normally keep hidden, suddenly reemerge when the relatives get together. The result is anger, anxiety, and depression.

Of course everyone isn't miserable at Christmas. Perhaps most of us are happy at this time of year, but there are two things the happy people must remember: (1) the potential for unhappiness is present in all of us, and (2) many of those around us *are* miserable at Christmas. In December these people need understanding, tolerance, and compassion, not criticism. God gave His Son to a saddened world on that first Christmas, and we too must give to others our time (short as it is), money, and interest. We can become so engrossed in the activities of our own Christmas that we easily overlook those who are not so happy.

What about this unhappy person? Can he or she do anything to bring the sparkle back into Christmas? Individuals can begin by pondering the Christ of Christmas and making time for worship. Then they can stop brooding in self-pity. This is not to deny reality if Christmas really hurts, but a good cure for holiday blues is to focus our attention on other people, help them, pray for them, and develop a positive mental attitude toward them.

My loneliest Christmas occurred one year when I was by myself in Germany. At 11:00

P.M. on Christmas Eve I slipped into a darkened Bavarian church for a candlelight service. We sang carols, listened to the Scriptures, and were reminded that Christ came as the light of the world. Near the end of the service two ushers walked down the aisle and each lit a candle from one lone candle on the altar. Then each member of the congregation was given a candle to light. Soon the previously darkened church became brilliant with the illumination of several hundred flickering flames. The congregation sang a carol as we marched out with our candles into a moonlit, snow-packed, crisp winter night. It was one of my most unforgettable Christmas experiences, and it served as a vivid reminder that the Christ who came to bring light to the world also is the antidote to Christmas misery.

6

The Mystery of Christmas

CHRISTMAS is a time for giving and receiving. Visit any shopping center in the middle of December, read a newspaper, or look under the tree on Christmas Eve, and the real focus of this holiday quickly becomes apparent. Christmas exists for the selling, buying, giving, receiving, and exchanging of gifts. Most of us would not want it any other way. Surprising each other with presents and trying to guess the contents of brightly decorated packages is part of the excitement that creates the fun of Christmas. Anticipating what we might get and wondering how our gifts to others will be received is part of the mystery of Christmas.

Giving can be a very pleasant experience. When we present a gift to someone, we are able in a tangible way to express our appreciation, respect, approval, sympathy, concern, or love. There is a real sense of satisfaction in discovering that we have made a good choice, that someone we love has been sincerely pleased with the selection that we have made.

But giving is not completely altruistic. Sometimes gifts are tainted with self-centered motives on the part of the giver. Gifts, for example, can be used to manipulate a receiver, making that person feel "bought" or put under obligation. Gifts from banks, businesses, or car dealers are sometimes of this type. They are used to buy good will and future sales from the receiver. At other times gifts are used to advance the giver's status either with the receiver or with someone else who will be impressed with the giver's affluence or good taste. The young suitor bearing roses and candy for his girl friend hopes that the gifts will advance his own status in the eyes of his beloved.

Gifts can also be used to relieve guilt. Parents who have ignored their children all year might buy expensive Christmas presents in a subconscious attempt both to dull the guilt they feel over their neglect and to buy the respect and love of their children. In addition, people give out of a sense of duty or habit. This is true especially at Christmas. Trapped into the habit of giving a lot of gifts to a lot of people, the harried shoppers run around trying to find something, almost anything, that will "do" for the various persons on their list. One man still remembers his parents buying so many gifts each year that they annually went into debt and spent all of the holidays complaining about how much Christmas cost.

The giving of gifts can hurt the receiver who is made to feel ashamed because he or she cannot or did not return a gift of equal value. At times we hurt people without realizing that we have done so, but on occasion this is done deliberately. I know of one divorced husband, for example, who gave a set of drums to his children who were living at the home of the giver's ex-wife!

In spite of these hidden motives on the part of some givers, each of us likes to receive presents. But even this receiving can create problems. We may have learned that it is more blessed to give than to receive; however, at times it may be more difficult to receive than to give. When we receive a present, we may not know what to say, especially if the gift is unexpected or unwanted. Gifts, as we have indicated, can put us under obligation to come up with a return gift of equal value or novelty. Sometimes a gift may even be humiliating. Paul Tournier, the famous Swiss writer, stated this concisely. "A beautiful gift," he wrote, "enhances the one who gives [but] . . . the gift which is too wonderful does not honor the one who receives; it humiliates him. One which goes beyond ordinary social conventions gives us quickly the feeling of being trapped, of becoming obligated to the giver, especially if we have no means of doing the same for him. In short, it alienates us."[7]

It is unlikely that many people think about all of this on Christmas morning or during the rush of holiday shopping, but it does appear that a lot of us become uptight about what to buy, how much to spend, whom to buy for, where to shop, and how we will pay the bills. With our concern about gifts we recast the famous Christmas story into a picture which is familiar in many homes:

> And there were in that same country, children keeping watch over their sox by firelight. And lo, Santa Claus came upon them; and the glory of his presence shown 'round about them, and they were sore enthralled.
>
> And Santa said unto them, "Fear not, for behold I bring you good tidings of great gifts which shall be to all people (with money to afford them). For unto you is cooked this day in the oven of your kitchen a turkey, which is surrounded by pudding and cakes and presents; and this shall be a sign unto you, ye shall find the gifts wrapped in

> sparkling paper and lying in a pile under the tree."
>
> And suddenly there was with the children a multitude of earthly relatives, praising each other and saying, "Thank you, this was just what I wanted."
>
> And it came to pass as Santa and the relatives were gone away into their own homes, the parents said one to another, "Let us now go even unto bed to avoid this mess which the kids and guests have made known unto us." And they came with haste and found peace, quiet and rest lying in a bed until morning.

The gift giving of Christmas often hides the fact that the first Christmas really centered around a gift, God's gift of His Son to mankind. God gave because He loved us. He had no other motive. He gave His Son so that we might believe on Him and have both eternal life after death and abundant life while we are here on earth.[8] Notice, however, that God never forced His gift on anyone. We can accept Christ into our lives or leave Him alone. According to the Bible, this Jesus was:

Revealed in the flesh,
Vindicated in the Spirit,
Beheld by angels,
Proclaimed among the nations,
Believed on in the world,
Taken up in glory.[9]

Little wonder that the Bible calls this a mystery. Why God should have sent His Son to a sinful world is a mystery far greater than that which surrounds the mysterious packages of Christmas.

At the time of the first Christmas, two groups of men came to visit the young Jesus. The wise men brought gifts of gold, frankincense, and myrrh, but so far as we can surmise the shepherds didn't bring anything. Nevertheless, both groups worshiped Christ. They gave themselves to the Son of God in dedication, praise, and obedience, and by this very act they also received the gift of life eternal. Even today this giving of oneself to Christ and this receiving of eternal life from Him are the greatest of all Christmas gifts.

7

The Master of Christmas

IN 1897 a little girl wrote to the *New York Sun* and asked if Santa Claus really existed. "Yes, Virginia," the newspaper editor replied in his now-famous editorial, "there is a Santa Claus!" In many respects and for many people this fat man with white beard and red suit has become the master symbol of Christmas.[10]

Nobody knows for sure how the Santa Claus legend got started, but it probably began with a Turkish bishop named Saint Nicholas who lived in the A.D. 300s. Bishop

Nicholas became famous for his generosity and kindness, especially to children, and during the Middle Ages he became the patron saint of schoolboys. Later the people of the Netherlands chose Saint Nicholas as the patron saint of Christmas, and each year in December a tall, thin man in bishop's robes and mitre rides in procession into Dutch communities to be welcomed by the children. During the night of his birthday, Saint Nicholas, or Sinterklaas as the Dutch children like to call him, is supposed to visit the homes of the children to leave presents and pick up the carrots and hay which have been left out for the saint's white horse.

When the Dutch settlers came to America in the 1600s, they brought the Saint Nicholas custom with them, and the British settlers quickly picked up the legends and festivities. It is not difficult to understand how English-speaking children took to the Dutch "Saint Nikolaas" or "Sinterklaas" and pronounced it "Santa Claus." As Santa's new name changed, so did his appearance. In America he ceased to be a tall, stately person; instead he began to look very much like the typical

Dutch settler in the state of New York: a plump, jolly fellow with hat and knee breeches. In 1822, when Clement C. Moore wrote his famous poem "A Visit from St. Nicholas," we see Santa Claus as the familiar "jolly" old man with a round figure, twinkling eyes, white beard, a nose like a cherry, and a bag full of toys slung on his back. A white horse had been replaced by "eight tiny reindeer" who were joined in the 1950s by a ninth reindeer named Rudolph, the creation of an advertising man at the Montgomery Ward Company in Chicago.

Santa Claus, more than anything else, has become the symbol of Christmas in the United States and other English-speaking countries like Canada, England, and Australia. Might it be, however, that in some homes Santa Claus has almost taken on the characteristics of an idol?

According to *Webster's New Collegiate Dictionary*, an idol is "an object of passionate devotion . . . an image or representation of a deity." For many children, and in the fantasy thinking of some adults, Santa Claus fits this description perfectly. That he is an "object of personal devotion" among many children is beyond dispute. That he is given divine characteristics is often forgotten.

Santa Claus is the giver of good and perfect gifts. Little children write him letters and come before him in department stores to let their requests be made known. All assume that Santa will bring many desirable presents.

Santa Claus is a source of great happiness. He is a jolly man who laughs heartily. For many he is *the* greatest source of happiness. He personifies the widely held belief that real joy comes with the acquisition of material possessions.

Santa Claus is omniscient and omnipresent. "He sees you when you're sleeping. He knows when you're awake. He knows if you've been bad or good." This is how he determines the number of gifts to bring.

Santa Claus is omnipotent. He is the only man in the world who can fly without mechanical help. He is pulled by a group of animals who also fly. He is able to visit every home in the world within a few hours and has the ability to get in and out of those homes, laden with toys, even when there are no fireplaces.

Santa Claus is a judge. "He's making a list, checking it twice," seeking to know "who's naughty and nice." The rewards are given on the basis of works.

For vast numbers of children, even in Christian homes, the Babe of Bethlehem has been replaced by a jolly, fat idol with red suit and white whiskers.

Realizing this, some Christian parents get carried away, perhaps in their opposition to Santa Claus. They refuse to have pictures of him in their homes and they deny their children the fun of seeing Santa Claus as a happy symbol of Christmas. Santa Claus need not be eliminated, but he needs to be kept in his proper place—a happy symbol of the season, not the master of Christmas.

As everyone knows, Christmas is a time of sleigh bells and holly wreaths, colored lights and Christmas trees, snowmen and candy canes. None of this is wrong. These things contribute to the wonder and excitement of Christmas. Even fantasy is desirable and healthy for little children. Sometimes, however, Christ, the true Master of Christmas, is replaced by these colorful holiday trappings. This *is* wrong! Since Santa Claus has become a pagan substitute for Christ, it is time that we dethroned him. The place to start is at home.

How do we dethrone Santa? Perhaps we begin by telling children the truth. No parents deliberately set out to deceive their children with stories about Santa Claus. We perpetuate the Santa Claus myth in order to make Christmas an even happier time for youngsters, but this may backfire. Children sometimes are crushed when they discover the truth about Santa, and it is difficult for them to separate fact from fiction if we later tell them that Jesus is real while Santa is a fake.

But how do you explain to a four-year-old that there is no Santa Claus? The problem will be handled differently in different homes and with different children, but the following is one approach:

"Santa Claus is a man dressed up in funny Christmas clothes. Some children believe he brings presents, but the toys that appear on Christmas morning are really put there by Mommy and Daddy. Some little children don't know that Santa Claus is just a man, so we must keep this a secret in our family."

With this should come an emphasis on the real meaning of Christmas. "It is the birthday of Jesus, and because it is a birthday, we give presents."

Even with this explanation, young children like to pretend that Santa Claus really does exist. Playing pretend games can be fun, as long as everyone realizes that we are "just pretending." Santa Claus is a delightful person, but he's a pretend person—not like Jesus Christ who came to be the real Master of Christmas.

8

The Miracles of Christmas

THE birth of Jesus on that first Christmas was a very unusual event. That a young girl should have a baby was not strange, of course. That there should be local interest in the baby's birth was also a normal occurrence. Such events have always been causes for celebration, expressions of joy, delight, and exclamations about the baby's beauty (even when the infant isn't remotely attractive).

The birth of Christ, however, was different from all the births which came before or after. So unique, in fact, are the events surrounding the first Christmas that many people refuse to believe, dismissing them as impossibilities; and others, while accepting the reality of the biblical accounts, conclude that the events really must be miracles.

Consider, for example, the *announcement* of Christ's coming. In the little Galilean town of Nazareth an angel reportedly appeared in visible form to tell an unmarried teenager that she was about to bear the child that devout followers of Judaism had been anticipating for centuries. More amazing than this, however, was the news about the *conception*. The child was to be conceived apart from any act of sexual intercourse. A virgin was to bear a child without first losing her virginity. Even the young girl Mary questioned this.[11] And when Joseph, her intended husband, discovered that Mary was pregnant, he made quiet plans to shield her from the scorn that was certain to follow.[12] Naturally, Joseph must have expected the worst (immorality or unfaithfulness) when he learned of Mary's condition, so another angel appeared, this time to explain to Joseph what was happening.

Almost as amazing as the announcements by the angels and the conception by the Holy Spirit was the *proclamation* by the heavenly hosts. Once again angels became visible—this time to a group of shepherds in the fields. At first there was one angel, then a huge choir appeared to sing the first and best known Christmas carol:

> Glory to God in the highest,
> And on earth peace among men
> with whom He is pleased.[13]

This was not all. There was the *revelation* of Christ's birth to a group of astronomers. This time no angel was involved, as far as we know, but the learned men saw a star which led them on a very long journey and brought them to the exact place where the young child and his parents were living.

Finally, there were the *circumstances* surrounding the baby's birth. Christ was supposed to be a king, but who ever heard of a king being born out of wedlock in a small stable, to a peasant-girl mother, and who was visited by a group of strangers whose job was to mind a flock of sheep? Little wonder that Mary pondered all of these things and thought about them "in her heart."[14]

Mary believed all of these things, as have generations of people since; but many have tried to explain it all away rationally and psychologically. We live in an age of skepticism. People are not inclined to believe anything which appears to come from God; and if they do believe in the supernatural, many prefer to put their faith in the horoscopes, ESP, Ouija boards, and the prophecies of astrologers. Many people today would rather believe in error than be caught dead acknowledging that the Bible stories might really be accurate accounts of history. It is not surprising, therefore, that attempts have been made to explain away the seemingly miraculous events of that first Christmas.

It has been argued, for example, that Mary saw not an angel but a hallucination. After all, she was young, not highly educated, very religious, and inclined to believe in the

supernatural. Joseph may have had a similar experience, and being in love he probably wanted desperately to believe that his future wife had not been unfaithful. A dream supporting Mary's story of the conception is certainly a feasible explanation of Joseph's vision. After the visit of the wise men, it is argued, Joseph had a premonition which led him to get his family up during the night and flee to Egypt.

It is more difficult to explain the shepherds' visions. These surely were not hallucinations. Hallucinations are private individual experiences that do not come to groups. One also wonders why the vision appeared only once, on the very night of Christ's birth, and led the shepherds to leave their sheep and go to a stable to visit a transient young couple and a tiny infant.

Modern astronomers have been able to account for the appearance of the star, but how could this heavenly body have led the wise men to a specific geographical location and why did they bring expensive gifts to strangers?

The biggest problem for the modern mind, however, is the virgin birth. It might be possible to find plausible explanations for the other Christmas events, but how do you explain conception and childbirth without prior sexual intercourse? Artificial insemination was unheard of in those days, and even if it had been, the Bible says it was the Holy Spirit, not medical technology, who caused the Christ child to appear in Mary's womb. Might it be that one must either believe in the miracle of the virgin birth on the basis of biblical evidence, or reject it? Most people reject it, including many who call themselves Christians and celebrate Christmas. "It's just impossible!" they conclude.

But is anything really impossible with God? Perhaps Christmas is a good season for us to ponder our view of God. Is He really all-powerful, all-knowing, loving, merciful, holy, and present everywhere? If so, He can do anything, including the virgin birth. If not, He is less than God and we worship a limited deity.

C.S. Lewis, in a little book on miracles, has suggested that God usually works through the natural world which He has created, but that sometimes He sidesteps the natural processes and does things in a highly unusual way. Consider, for example, the time when Jesus turned water into wine at the wedding in Cana.

> Every year, as part of the natural order, God makes wine. He does so by creating a vegetable organism that can turn water, soil, and sunlight into a juice which will, under the proper condi-

> tions, become wine. Thus, in a certain sense, he constantly turns water into wine, for wine, like all drinks, is but water modified. Once, and in one year only, God, now incarnate, short circuits the process; makes wine in a moment; uses earthenware jars instead of vegetable fibers to hold the water. But uses them to do what he is always doing. The miracle consists in the short cut; but the event to which it leads is a usual one.[15]

A similar short-circuiting of nature must have occurred at the time of Christ's conception. Every child who has been conceived, except one, began life as the result of sexual intercourse. Once, however, God decided to bypass this natural order. He created life in the same way that all of us have been created except that the act of sexual intercourse was eliminated.

It is not surprising that some people are skeptical about this. Skepticism in itself isn't a bad thing. By our being skeptical and raising questions, science and technology have made great advances. But too much skepticism can lead to despair, emptiness, cynicism, and unwillingness to believe in anything. For many people Christmas has become a big celebration, but a celebration of nothing. Perhaps we need to look again at the miracles of Christmas. They show us what we are really commemorating at this season, and they point us to the real message of Christmas.

9

The Message of Christmas

WHAT is the message of Christmas, the real meaning of this holiday which we celebrate each December?

Many years before the birth of Christ, the Old Testament prophets had predicted that at some time in the future the Lord would "give you a sign: Behold, a virgin will be with child and bear a son, and she will call His name Immanuel. . . . And His name will be called Wonderful Counselor, Mighty God, Eternal Father, Prince of Peace."[16] God had decided, centuries before the first

Christmas, to send His Son to earth in the form of a man.

But why would God want to do that? After the birth of Christ the Apostle Paul commented on the reasons for Christ's coming. "It is a trustworthy statement, deserving full acceptance, that Christ Jesus came into the world to save sinners."[17] Those who believe in Him, Paul added, have the assurance of eternal life. Little wonder that the Apostle followed this observation with a hymn of praise:

> Now to the King eternal, immortal, invisible, the only God, be honor and glory forever and ever. Amen.[18]

Undoubtedly the best known and most concise summary of the message of Christmas came in the angel's message to the shepherds: "Today in the city of David there has been born for you a Savior, who is Christ the Lord."[19] Notice the three little words that are used to describe the baby: Savior, Christ, and Lord.

A *savior* is someone who rescues a needy person when that person is unable to rescue himself. According to the Bible, and our own common sense, none of us is perfect. We have all sinned, but this presents us with a double problem: God is holy and cannot look on sin, but we are powerless to rescue ourselves from sin's clutches. God, therefore, sent His Son to rescue us and to restore us to wholeness and communion with God.

The title *Christ* means "anointed one." In the Bible, and some modern countries like England, oil is used to touch the head of a designated ruler as a mark of the ruler's kingship. Christ, therefore, came as a king. His very name indicates the purpose of His coming: not only to save us but to establish a kingdom. At this point in history He is inviting us to pay homage to Him, and someday He will return in splendor with His subjects, to rule and to reign in supremacy as king.

Lord is a term which implies absolute sovereignty. If Christ is Lord, as He claims, then we must give Him our complete obedience, just as God on the first Christmas gave Christ completely to mankind.

This, then, is the real message of Christmas, the real reason for our celebration. In response to God's ancient promise, a Savior has come to earth to restore mankind to communion with God and personal completeness.

It is interesting that so many of the Christmas celebrants miss all of this. They go about their celebration without realizing that the King of the universe is waiting for some personal response from them. Most people are simply indifferent to Christ, some have a casual interest in Him, many reject Him outright, and only a few give Him the absolute obedience that His kingship demands.

Those who submit to the Christ of Christmas can make only one response—praise. Mary sang a hymn of praise on that first Christmas and so did the angels, the shepherds, the wise men, the aged Simeon and

Anna, the unborn John the Baptist, Mary's elderly cousin Elizabeth and her husband Zacharias. When we realize the real message of Christmas, we will join our voices to the chorus.

A thought-provoking Christmas card shows the picture of a discouraged young man sitting in the midst of Christmas tree decorations and unwrapped boxes. "When you get right down to it," the message proclaims, "the only thing that really matters is Jesus!" Simple as it may seem, this is the real message of Christmas.

10

The Merriment of Christmas

THE custom of sending Christmas cards probably began in London in 1843 when the first specially designed card was put on the market. Within twenty years the idea had caught on in England, but it wasn't until 1875 that Christmas cards were sold and exchanged in America.

Cards now differ greatly in terms of quality, design, and message. They do much to reflect the personality, beliefs, economic status, and values of the sender, although most of us do not think about this when the mailman arrives during the days of mid-December. There is one thing, however, that almost all Christmas cards have in common. They convey some kind of greeting and wish for happiness at the holiday season. We send them to wish one another a merry Christmas.

But how can we expect to be merry in a world that is in political and economic chaos? How can we be merry when thousands are suffering from acute famine and the ravages of war? How can people be merry at a season of the year when we are

rushed off our feet with busyness and prone to get discouraged? Where is there reason to be merry in a society where people refuse to believe in God's sovereignty, doubt His power to perform miracles, and ignore the message of His angels who proclaimed the good news of Christ's birth?

It is not easy to cope with Christmas, but real merriment *is* possible, especially if we follow a few simple guidelines.

First, we can make a deliberate effort to *reduce the holiday pressures* on ourselves and others. We can start our preparations early, eliminate what really does not need to be done, and plan activities that will focus on the real meaning of Christmas, the birth of God's Son. Most of the busyness of Christmas is our own fault. It comes because of poor planning, procrastination, or disorganization, and it tends to crowd out Christ. Perhaps we need to be more realistic in making Christmas plans and more willing to pace ourselves accordingly. We need to avoid overextending and overcommitting ourselves lest we try to do too much and end up by being frustrated because we have failed. Perhaps as part of our planning we need to spend more time considering how we can be still at Christmas and know that He is God.

Second, each of us might be more alert to the needs of others and aware of *ways in which we could help* those who are lonely, discouraged, or in special need at Christmas. This may mean giving of our time, money, and energy to make others feel wanted and remembered. It may mean opening our homes to others and sharing Christmas or giving to those who have less than we do. Every Christmas we spend so many dollars on gifts and food for our own families but so little on others who are lonely or needy.

A seminary student recently described the first Christmas he and his wife had celebrated as a married couple. "Actually," he said, "we had three Christmases—one by ourselves, one with our parents, and one with a needy family whose name we received through a community agency. The family had nothing, not even chairs to sit on. We took them a decorated tree, a turkey, and presents for the kids." Such a giving, sharing attitude cannot fail to gladden the heart of the giver at Christmas.

Third, we can give special consideration to *what we are teaching* our children at Christmas. Saying little about the Christ of Christmas, overstressing frenzied activity or the receiving of gifts, teaching children a devotion to Santa Claus, doing nothing to minister to the needs of others—these are all ways in which we teach children that Christmas is something other than a celebration of Christ's coming. Parents might talk about keeping Christ in Christmas, but to children actions always speak louder than words.

This leads us to a fourth suggestion. Each of us must actively *draw near to God* at Christmas. Caught up in the holiday season, we easily let our devotional life slip and even forget temporarily about religious things. But a Christ-centered, merry Christmas is not likely to come automatically. It comes when we plan ahead and deliberately make room for Christ in our holiday celebrations and make Him the center of our holidays.

11

The Memories of Christmas

HAVE you ever heard of post-Christmas depression? That term might not mean much to some, but it refers to an experience which is very common—the feeling of a great letdown after the holidays.

Many people reach Christmas Day in a state of near exhaustion from weeks of gift buying, party planning, card writing, socializing, and general anticipatory tension. Finally the magic day arrives. We open our presents, eat our turkey, participate in our church services, visit and entertain friends, take part in all of the Christmas traditions—and suddenly everything is over. The colored lights are turned off, the tree comes down, the decorations are put away, and Christmas is gone for another year.

In one sense this brings a feeling of relief. The pressure is off and we are able to settle once again into our normal routines of life. As we do so, however, there is also a sense of nostalgia, a reluctance to see it all end. For many there is also discouragement and depression, a post-Christmas depression.

Psychiatrists have suggested a number of reasons why people get discouraged after the holidays. Sometimes there is exhaustion from all of the activity, grogginess from overindulgence, boredom at the thought of returning to work, and discouragement at the contemplation of a long dreary winter ahead. Some people are jolted by the annual realization that the happy "Christmas spirit" was temporary, that nothing has really changed in their faltering marriages, strained family relationships, or difficulties with colleagues at work. Add to this the reality of January bills and the realization for many that it is time to go on a diet to take off extra Christmas pounds, and we begin to see why almost everyone, even well-adjusted personalities, suffer pangs of post-holiday blues, at least temporarily.

For some people, like those who are predisposed to severe depression, the holidays can be tragic. One of the directors of the Los Angeles Suicide Prevention Center has stated that "really bad depressions and suicides hit on the second, third and fourth of January. . . . It's the worst week of the year."[20]

Happily, most of us don't get depressed enough to even ponder suicide after Christmas. We pick up our daily schedules and go on, sorry perhaps that the excitement is over but glad to be back in the old routine again.

This apparently was what happened after the first Christmas. The angels went back to heaven, the shepherds went back to work, the wise men went back to their own country, and Joseph took Mary and the child back to Nazareth (after a sojourn in Egypt). We can only guess about Anna and Simeon, but presumably they died shortly after the birth of Christ. The young Jesus became strong and grew in wisdom. All of these participants in the first Christmas went back to their regular routines of life, but one never has the impression that these people experienced a post-holiday depression. For them Christmas had not been the *end* of a round of busy activities. For them Christmas was the *beginning* of a new life-style. They returned to work as usual, but some things doubtless were different.

First, there probably was a *new attitude* towards God, an attitude of praise, worship, and thanksgiving. Post-Christmas depression (like much other depression) comes when we focus attention on ourselves, wallow in self-pity and develop a "poor-little-me" attitude. Discouragement is almost inevitable when our own problems, boredom, and meaninglessness become the main focus of our attention. The people at that first Christmas would have agreed with the words of a hymn written centuries later:

> Turn your eyes upon Jesus
> Look full in His wonderful face
> And the things of earth will grow strangely dim
> In the light of His glory and grace.[21]

It could be argued that this is escapism, avoiding the reality of life's problems by forgetting them as we praise God. But to worship God in spite of circumstances can help us to see things in a new, broader perspective. The men and women who saw the Christ child pondered what they had seen, praised God for His love in sending His Son, and worshiped in a spirit of gratitude.

Second, the coming of Christ was followed by a *new peace*. The King James Version of the Bible has created a false impression of the angels' song to the shepherd. The message was not "peace on earth, good will to men"; the message was "peace among men with whom He is pleased." Peace was not promised to everyone. It was promised only to those who please God.

How does one please God? Worshiping Him is one way; confessing our sins and committing our lives to Him is another. Notice the Bible's words on this issue. "Without faith," we read, "it is impossible to please Him for he who comes to God must believe that He is, and that He is a rewarder of those who seek Him."[22] Inner peace, the peace that lasts beyond Christmas and throughout the new year, comes only to those who believe that God exists and put their faith in Him. The requirement for real peace is demanding, and few are willing to pay the price.

In addition to peace and praise, the participants in that first Christmas showed *a new obedience*. For these people, obedience to God wasn't all that new. Mary, Joseph, Simeon, Anna, the shepherds, and wise men had all shown a willingness to obey God long before they met the Christ child. Perhaps this willing attitude was one of the reasons why they were privileged to see the child in the first place. But after Christmas these people continued to obey. The wise men obeyed God's instructions to go to their "own country by another way," and Simeon showed a willingness to be taken in death now that he had seen the baby. His prayer in the Temple contains elements of praise, the experience of peace, and a willingness to obey—all in a couple of sentences.

> Now Lord, Thou dost let Thy (obedient) bondservant depart
> In peace, according to Thy word;
> For mine eyes have seen Thy salvation,
> Which Thou hast prepared in the presence of all peoples.[23]

Notice that Simeon's life had been lived according to God's Word. The first step in obedience to God is to read and obey His Word, the Bible. This is both a good New Year's resolution and an important step in avoiding the post-holiday depression.

A *new outreach* was the fourth response of the early Christians. After seeing the Christ child the shepherds did not keep things to themselves. They told everybody.[24] So did Anna[25] and so, it might be presumed, did Simeon, the wise men, Elizabeth, and Zacharias. At the end of His life, immediately before ascending into heaven, Jesus reemphasized the importance of reaching out to others. Go into the world and make disciples, He said, winning people to Christ and teaching them to grow spiritually.

A radio commentator once described the Christmas season as a time for happiness, gift giving, and joy. It transcends race, status, and creed. She said, "Christmas is a holiday for Christians, Moslems, atheists, and agnostics. It is greater than any religion."

Who is this lady trying to fool? Christmas without Christ is a sham, an empty holiday which is organized in a way that will guarantee disappointment and post-holiday despair. In contrast, Christmas for the follower of Christ is an annual reminder of what Christ has done and is doing *for* us, and what He expects *of* us.

The days after Christmas need not be a time to mope, wallow in misery, and mull over the memories of a holiday season which is past. Instead, Christmas should launch us into a period of new adoration, new peace, new obedience, and a new outreach to others. The real spirit of Christmas should begin when the celebrating stops.

Notes

1. From an interview with Canadian psychiatrist Dr. Giampiero Bartolucci. Reported in *The Spectator*, January 19, 1974.

2. Many of the ideas in this chapter are adapted from an article by James Montgomery Boice, "The Men Who Missed Christmas," *Christianity Today*, December 9, 1972, pp. 4-5.

3. In one sense Xmas does not take the Christ out of Christmas. Christ comes from the Greek χριστός, but most of us who are not Greek scholars do not think of this when we write "Merry Xmas."

4. The ideas expressed in this paragraph and throughout the chapter were presented previously in an article by the author. See Gary R. Collins, " 'Tis the Season to Be Jolly—Or Melancholy," *Christianity*

Today, December 7, 1973, pp. 5-6.

5. John T. Wallace, Jr., "The Dark Side of Christmas," *Eternity*, December, 1973, pp. 12-13,45.

6. Ruth Rondy, "Let's Hear It for Scrooge," *The Milwaukee Journal*, December 24, 1972.

7. Paul Tournier, *The Meaning of Gifts* (Richmond: John Knox Press, 1963), p. 28.

8. John 3:16; 10:10.

9. 1 Timothy 3:16.

10. Much of this chapter is adapted from the article by Gary R. Collins, "It's Time We Straightened Virginia Out," *Eternity*, December, 1972, p. 18.

11. Luke 1:34.

12. Matthew 1:19.

13. Luke 2:14.

14. Luke 2:19.

15. C.S. Lewis, *Miracles* (London: Collins Fontana Books, 1947), p. 140.

16. Isaiah 7:14; 9:6.

17. 1 Timothy 1:15.

18. 1 Timothy 1:17.

19. Luke 2:11.

20. "Coping with Depression," *Newsweek*, January 8, 1973, pp. 51-54.

21. "Turn Your Eyes Upon Jesus," by Helen H. Lemmel. Copyright 1922. Renewal 1950 by Helen H. Lemmel. Assigned to Singspiration, Inc. All rights reserved. Used by permission.

22. Hebrews 11:6.

23. Luke 2:29-31.

24. Luke 2:17.

25. Luke 2:38.

About the Author

Gary R. Collins is professor of psychology and chairman of the Division of Pastoral Counseling and Psychology at Trinity Evangelical Divinity School in Deerfield, Illinois. Following studies in Canada and England, Collins earned his Ph.D. degree in clinical psychology at Purdue University.

A prolific writer, Dr. Collins has authored or edited almost thirty books, including *How to Be a People Helper, Spotlight on Stress, Calm Down,* and *Helping People Grow: Practical Approaches to Christian Counseling.*

Dr. Collins resides in northern Illinois with his wife and two daughters.